BIG BENCH

"basics, 'breviated and best"

WARNING

This course stresses the importance of using proper technique and safety when using a bodybuilding or strength training program. Check with your health practitioner to ensure that it's appropriate for you to follow such a program. Follow the instructions carefully. Neither the authors nor CS Publishing Ltd. will be responsible for any physical injury that may result from following the routines and advice given in this course.

BIG BENCH Copyright © 1993 by Brooks D. Kubik and Stuart McRobert. All rights reserved. Cover illustration work by Eleni Lambrou, Copyright © 1993.

Published by CS Publishing Ltd., P.O. Box 8186, Nicosia – CYPRUS.

Printed in Cyprus by Zavallis Litho Ltd.

WHERE WE STAND

We are dedicated to providing the most consistent, practical, hype-free and undiluted source of training information for typical, hard-gaining, drug-free bodybuilders and power trainees. (While this bench press course is primarily aimed at powerlifters and bodybuilders, our publications also provide instruction for function-first strength athletes.) Though our focus is always upon training methods that work for genetically-typical people, the instruction we promote works even better for those blessed with better-than-average genetics.

While everyone can get stronger than they are now, and most people can get *much* stronger, and while some of you will develop very impressive strength *and* a very impressive physique, the spectacular levels (that of professional and top amateur competitors) can only belong to a minuscule minority. Such achievement necessitates extraordinary genetics *plus* heavy and long-term use of performance-enhancing drugs. This is the reality, no matter how persuasive some advertising copy, article, book or word-of-mouth statements to the contrary may be. If you have good genetics and fierce determination, you may eventually win drug-free powerlifting meets, but you will *never* be able to compete with the genetically gifted who train hard *and* are on the "juice."

The irony of bodybuilding and powerlifting is that the training methods generally promoted to the masses only deliver good results for those who are *extraordinarily* blessed genetically, or for those who use drugs to compensate for genetic shortcomings. Advice that emanates from the drug-assisted and/or the genetically gifted almost always has nothing, and I mean *NOTHING*, to do with what's needed by typical, drug-free bodybuilders and powerlifters. Any training advice taken from that source usually causes training "suicide" for the hard gainer.

This bench press course gives a "taste" of what effective training methods for typical trainees are about. Yes they fly in the face of conventional gym instruction, but they need to because conventional training instruction has an appalling failure rate. Have a look around any typical gym. Take away the drug users and the few naturals who can get big and very strong virtually no matter how they train, and you will be left with no really big and strong guys in almost every gym you visit.

Conventional weight training is distinguished by the almost universal application of training methods that produce little or no gains for most drug-free users. Most bodybuilders train for years with only minimal results. They waste their time with puny poundages and useless programs. Even most powerlifters fail to train effectively. Some advanced lifters may move respectable weights, but even they usually get stuck at the same poundages for years.

Our publications are about:
1. More practical, instruction-dense, time-proven training advice for typical, drug-free people than can be found anywhere else.

2. Radical opinions telling you what you need to hear, not just what you may want to hear.

3. Training methods that actually work without great genetics and without drug assistance; methods that will get you on the road towards a 400-pound squat, a 300 bench press and a 500 deadlift, and then *beyond* if you have the motivation, persistence, body structure and patience.

4. Training routines that rely mostly upon traditional and commonly available equipment.

5. Paramount concern for grassroots trainees, not for the genetically-gifted and drug-using minority that usually receives almost all of the attention.

6. Step-by-step training programs for beginners, intermediates and advanced bodybuilders, plus challenging but realistic targets.

7. Material written by typical, *drug-free* people, and instruction that keeps in mind that few people are free of demanding work and family responsibilities—most people just can't adopt a live-in-the-gym devotion to training.

Through HARDGAINER (a magazine published by CS Publishing Ltd., since July 1989) there are consistent, bimonthly reminders of how to keep on the training "straight and narrow," with a variety of authors providing their views.

Bodybuilding and powerlifting are not the mysterious, complicated, time consuming and expensive activities like many would have you believe. You can achieve miracles with only the very basic equipment, only a few hours of training each week, ordinary but nutritious food, and without needing to buy any food supplements (though using some quality supplements in the second half of each cycle may give you a nutritional boost at the right time). The essence of our message is "basics, 'breviated and best," which is what this course for a big bench press is all about. Actually, "basics and 'breviated" is not only "best," it's the *only* way to go for most drug-free bodybuilders and lifters.

Getting substantially bigger and stronger is about using progressive poundages—a bit more, a bit more again, and then a bit more again and again and again..., while *always* maintaining good exercise form. (Religiously keep written records of your workouts, to keep track of your poundages, reps and sets.) The exercises that matter the most are the big, basic "building" exercises, i.e., the multi-joint "compound" exercises, not the little isolation exercises. Conventional bodybuilding has mesmerized and distracted people with inordinate amounts of writing and attention being given to marginal, incidental or irrelevant concerns. Even powerlifters usually spend too much time on non-productive "assistance" exercises. All the attention in the world to the variety of different training modalities, different rep cadences, different set and rep schemes, "scientific" and "physiological" rationales, isolation or "detail" exercises, "new" exercises, supplement "discoveries," personalities, contests, videos, training camps and seminars count for *absolutely nothing* unless you are adding more and more iron to the bar, *in good form*, as the months and years go by. If you are not, then, like hundreds of thousands of others, you are just getting more and more knowledgeable about everything and anything except that which will actually make you grow bigger and stronger.

Once you are beyond the beginner stage of bodybuilding and powerlifting, the bedrock of progressive poundages is the cycling of training intensity. *Always* trying to add poundage to your limit working poundages *is not* the way to go. Instead, train in periods (cycles) where you cut back at the beginning of each cycle (to get a "running start") and take several weeks—adding 5-10 pounds per week to each exercise—until getting to within 10-15 pounds of the best poundages you were using before starting the new cycle, for whatever reps you are using. Then, get hold of a selection of little discs of varying small weights: half pound, one pound, 100 grams, 250 grams and 500 grams, or use improvised weights of light collars, large metal washers or even taping small pieces of iron onto bigger plates. Use these to notch up your exercise weights so slightly that you don't feel you are adding weight.

Take a further few weeks to get to your most recent best working poundages. Once there, keep adding a very small dose of iron to the bar every week. You can build strength for perhaps months at a time if you keep adding a tiny dose of iron each week. However, if you get impatient and try to keep adding 5 or more pounds a week, you will "kill" the "gaining momentum" because you will be adding iron at a rate in excess of your body's ability to build strength. Slowly, steadily, surely and safely is the way to go. Once the poundage gains finally "dry up," end the cycle, layoff for 7-10 days, cut back your poundages, perhaps change something in your routine for the sake of change and variety, and then build up again. Each cycle should have you starting a little higher than did the previous one, and have you finishing at higher poundages than did the previous one. (There are many ways to cycle training intensity—extensive detail on it can be found in BRAWN. See the ad for this book on the rear inside cover of this course.)

Part of the reality message we promote is believable measurements and lifts. Much fiction is presented as fact in the training world, including absurd measurement and lift claims by some of the most genetically gifted and "juiced" top achievers. For typical and drug-free bodybuilders, here are some reality-land measurements you should be looking at—a muscular and flexed 16" upper arm is very good, 17" is astonishing, and over 17" is fantastic. For a typical, drug-free powerlifter, a bench press of 300-320 pounds is very good, 340-360 is astonishing, and anything over 375 is fantastic. Those who can hit 400 pounds without bodybuilding drugs are supermen.

Read - Understand - Apply - Persist - Achieve

Stuart McRobert
Director
CS Publishing Ltd.

FLYNN AND THE BENCH PRESS KING

I have often thought it was a pity that Flynn's parents lacked the foresight to name their son Adam, Bob, Charlie or some other name that began with one of the earlier letters in the alphabet. Had they done so, the name of the gym would have appeared at the beginning of the gym listings in the telephone book. Then, more people would have come to Flynn's gym at the start of their training careers rather than after wasting months or even years in some of the other "training" establishments throughout the city. My pondering, on the vast number of people who waste years of their training lives, was interrupted by the arrival of the Bench Press King.

Charlie is a 22-year old who had spent the first four years of his training career at one of the other gyms in town. He came to Flynn's gym only after being stuck at 180 pounds in the bench press for a full year.

"You should have seen him when he first came in, nearly two years ago," Flynn told me. "He stood 5'10", weighed 160 pounds. Said he wanted to bench press 300 pounds and that he would die trying. Told me about his training routine. You can guess what it was like. Worked his chest five days a week; did his one-rep max most days; did 20 or 25 sets of regular benches, 10 sets of inclines, 5 sets of declines, 10 sets of cable crossovers, 10 sets on the pec deck (the last 3 with negative resistance to end the sets), flat bench and incline flyes for 5 sets each, and 10 or 15 sets of tricep pushdowns. Did lat work maybe once a week—did curls once in a while—and never did anything else. Hadn't done a squat or deadlift in three years. Ate like a bird and spent most of his money on some amino optimizer they sell in pseudo gyms for $40 a can."

"I bet he asked what you thought about his training program," I replied.

Flynn laughed. "He sure did. I told him that it was Sunday and I couldn't properly express myself on the subject of his training program without breaking my New Year's resolution about cursing on Sundays. Believe me, giving him the nickname of the Bench Press King was the least harsh of my comments."

CHARLIE'S FIRST PROGRAM AT FLYNN'S GYM

Flynn walked over to the filing cabinet where he keeps a training file on all of his members. He found the kid's file and pulled out the first training program he mapped out for the kid:

Monday
1. Squat: 5 x 5
2. Bench press: 5 x 5
3. Pulldown: 5 x 5
4. Crunch sit-up: 1 x 30

Wednesday
1. Press behind neck (seated): 5 x 5
2. Barbell curl: 5 x 5
3. Standing calf raise: 2 x 10
4. Crunch sit-up: 1 x 30

Friday
1. Squat: 5 x 5 (use only 80% of the top weight used on Monday)
2. Close-grip bench (16" grip): 5 x 5
3. Deadlift: 5 x 5

"I see what you planned to do in this routine," I told Flynn. "You wanted to get the kid working on all the major body parts, not just his chest. In particular, you wanted him to start doing some squatting. You used a 5 x 5 system because the kid's marathon workouts were volume intensive, not weight intensive, and he wasn't ready to do any low-rep training. The 5 x 5 system is a good way to transition from high reps to the type of low-rep power training that really builds strength." Flynn grunted, which I took as some sort of general agreement with my assessment.

To use the 5 x 5 system, you do 2 progressively heavier warmup sets followed by 3 sets of 5 reps with your "working weight." As the cycle progresses, the working sets will get harder to do and eventually will be as heavy as you can possibly manage. If 5 x 5 is too tough, do just 4 x 5—only 2 sets with the top weight.

It was hard to sell the kid on working out three days a week, and particularly hard to sell him on training his bench press only two times per week. So instead of having him do press behind neck on Monday, and curls on Friday, Flynn put those into a Wednesday workout, to get the kid to the gym on a third day each week.

CHARLIE'S SECOND PROGRAM

Flynn was flipping through Charlie's training file, looking for the second workout program. "There it is!" He handed me the program—every time he hands me something I have the impression that I'm reaching out to shake hands with a gorilla—and I looked it over.

Charlie's second training program was, like the first, a twelve-week program.

Monday
1. Squat: 5 x 5
2. Bench press: 2 x 5 (progressively heavier warmups), then 5/4/3/2/1
3. Bent-over row: 5 x 5
4. Crunch sit-up: 1 x 40

Wednesday
1. Seated dumbbell press: 4 x 6
2. Incline dumbbell curl: 4 x 6
3. Seated calf raise: 2 x 10
4. Side bend: 1 x 15 (each side)

Friday
1. Deadlift: 5 x 5
2. Bench press: 4 x 5
3. Pulldown: 4 x 5
4. Incline (30°) dumbbell press: 4 x 5
5. Crunch sit-up: 1 x 40

"The 5/4/3/2/1 system in the bench-press is the second step in moving from moderate-rep or high-rep training, to true low-rep training," said Flynn.

I nodded—I had heard it before. I had tried it before, in fact. Charlie wasn't the only guy in the gym who had profited from Flynn's instruction.

"The way to do the system is to start with a couple of warmup sets and then do 5 working sets. The first will be a weight that makes you work to do 5 reps, but not your absolute maximum for 5—that would leave you too tired to do any more work on that exercise. Use a weight that makes you put forth a good effort. Then add a bit of weight and do 4 reps. Shoot for the same sort of intensity—hard, but not impossible. Add weight and do a set of 3. Then more weight, for a double. More weight, and a single. The triple, double and single will not be true maximum attempts because you will be a little tired from having done the set of 5 and the set of 4. That's intentional—keeps you from going too heavy too soon and outrunning your body's ability to toughen up."

"You didn't have him use his top weights from the very start, did you?"

"No, of course not. In all of Charlie's programs, he started comfortably and built up the poundages so that he wasn't training flat out until about the sixth week. This left him with about six weeks of very hard work in each program. You can't train flat out all the time, remember. That's real important—and it applies to *every* training program you do. It's critical to start slow and gradually work up to your best weights in each cycle you do."

"What kind of results did Charlie get?"

"He surprised me," said Flynn. "I knew that once he got off the five-day-a-week benching program he would put at least 10 pounds on his best bench, and I knew that cutting down to heavy sets of 5 done just once a week would make the lift jump another 10 pounds. But Charlie outdid himself. He worked hard on all of his lifts, particularly the squats and deadlifts, and at the end of the first twelve-week program when I let him go for a heavy max, he was able to push 210. Remember, this was a kid who had been stuck at 180 pounds for a whole year. Then he took a one-week layoff and repeated the first program for a second twelve-week cycle—which pushed his one-rep max to 225 pounds. He also gained seven pounds of muscle during the first cycle and another five pounds during the second cycle. That really helped him. It's almost impossible for a rookie to greatly increase his bench press without adding a substantial amount of muscular bodyweight."

"How did he respond to the second program?" I asked.

"After using the program for twelve weeks, he gained five more pounds of muscle and ended up pushing 240. After a one-week layoff, he did the program again and ended up hitting a 250-pound max.

"All in all, Charlie added twenty pounds of muscle and 70 pounds to his bench in the first year at our gym," Flynn continued. "That's terrific progress. Most guys would be lucky to do even half as well. But Charlie had been using an idiot program for so long that his body was just waiting for a sensible system. He *had* to respond to the proper approach.

"In addition, Charlie worked real hard on his form. Benching big weights calls for good biomechanics and lots of work on technique. We taught him to lift with his feet flat on the floor—butt firmly against the bench, shoulders ditto—and to push up and *back*, in a good arc. Remember, the bar moves both vertically *and* horizontally when you bench. You need to push the bar up and then back towards your face, not just straight up over the chest. At the completion of the lift, the bar should be over your eyes or even an inch or so further back.

"We also taught Charlie to lower the bar at a fairly slow, controlled speed, and to hit the right spot on his chest at the bottom of every rep—just below the nipples for most guys. Before trying our system, Charlie used to drop the bar as fast as possible and bounce it up off of his chest—a terrific way to injure yourself and a lousy way to build strength. We made Charlie train with a two-second pause on each and every rep. This is the best way in the world to build real benching power. Leave the fast drops and the bounces to the clowns who want to trade momentary ego satisfaction for chronic shoulder problems.

"Charlie was used to lifting his butt three or four inches on each rep, to help get the bar up. We taught him to keep his butt on the bench and to use a proper arch instead. All top benchers use an arch, to raise their chests in order to reduce the range of pressing motion. Using an arch also makes it easier to push the bar up and back. In other words, it promotes a proper bar path. Of course, when you arch, you keep your butt on the bench—lifting your butt will get you disqualified in competition—so when we say 'arch,' we mean to position yourself so your hips and shoulders are as close as possible while still touching the bench.

"The kid was used to benching on an empty chest, so we trained him to take a huge breath before each rep, lower the bar with his chest full of air, and exhale forcefully as he hit the sticking point when pushing the bar up.

"We also changed his grip. Like many novices, he was using too-wide a grip for his body structure. We switched him to one where his elbows were directly under and in line with his hands at the bottom of the lift. That works best for most guys.

"Charlie also started to use a bar with deep knurling and to *dust* his hands with chalk before lifting. He had been using a smooth bar at his old gym—the manager over there likes the smooth bars because his members don't want calluses on their hands. If your bar lacks heavy knurling, you can wrap some heavy tape around it—that will always help your grip. Just be sure to use a solid, tight grip with chalk on your hands, to be able to have as firm a hold of the bar as possible. This is necessary for safety and, also, it helps to promote confidence—makes you *feel* a lot stronger, and that's half the battle. Also, we got the kid off the dangerous 'thumbless grip' he was using and onto the safe and solid thumbs-around-the-bar-and-touching-index-fingers style that all members at Flynn's Gym use.

"We also taught Charlie the elbows-against-the-lats technique. Most guys bench with their upper arms perpendicular to the torso, i.e., with the elbows in line with the shoulders. This position greatly weakens your benching power. What you want to do is to bench with the lats flexed, pulling the upper arms in tight against the torso as you lower the bar. Your arms should caress your sides as the weight comes down. This means that your powerful lat muscles will be supporting the weight at the bottom. Then, when you start to press, begin by exploding the lats—push the weight up in the first few inches of movement by a combined arm, shoulder, chest and lat drive.

"Another thing we had to see to was Charlie's approach to resting between sets. Before coming to Flynn's Gym, he rushed between sets—but we soon fixed that. We got him taking 3-5 minutes between his heavy sets, and even longer between his end-of-cycle very heavy sets."

"What about support gear?" I asked.

"Charlie wasn't ready for it," said Flynn. "I had him use a belt, of course—that helps prevent injury at any level of a power training program. He ordered the belt from a company that sells for powerlifters—no pseudo-stuff. Use a 4" wide, double-thickness leather power belt. Don't waste money on cheap gear. It was too early though to start him on the bench shirt. Unless you use the shirt because of an old injury, save it for *after* you go over the 300 or 350-pound mark under your own steam. You will build a much better muscular base that way. Ditto for wrist wraps—save them for *after* you can handle 300 pounds. And even when you are advanced, consider training *without* any support gear other than a belt. Many guys build more strength that way, and get a big 'boost' when they put on a shirt and wrist wraps in competition. Whatever you do, don't become dependent on support gear.

"Charlie also increased his overall strength by changing to a sensible diet. He had practically been living on food supplements, tuna fish and egg whites. We taught him to eat three or four well-balanced meals every day, basing his diet on lean meat, chicken, turkey, fish, eggs, milk, cheese, bread, potatoes, rice, spaghetti, fresh fruit and fresh vegetables. You can't eat like a sparrow and expect to be as strong as a bear.

"All in all, I would say that Charlie's progress was primarily due to the fact that he switched to a sensible program—but also due to the form work he did, to the new diet he followed, and to his extra bodyweight.

"If he had not responded well to the new diet and the new program, I would have *reduced* his workload. I would have had him try 3 x 5 on benches and squats, twice per week, and nothing else. That would be 2 warmup sets and one heavy set for each exercise. That program will get anyone going. Remember, if you are not getting the results you want, try doing *less* work before you try doing *more*. That works better in 99 cases out of 100."

CHARLIE'S THIRD PROGRAM

"What kind of program did the kid use next?" I asked.

"Another of my old favorites," said Flynn. "A short, simple, but incredibly effective program. Here it is—and it's a sure-fire winner once you have developed the tolerance to do the low-rep training by using programs one and two for two cycles each, and as long as you don't jump immediately into using your top weights. Start with comfortable poundages and pick up the weights gradually over about six weeks. Then, over the final six weeks of the cycle, push hard to increase your weights in all exercises."

Monday
1. Squat: 4 x 5 (warmups), then 2 x 5 (heavy).
2. Seated calf raise: 2 x 10-15.
3. Crunch sit-up with a dumbbell on the chest: 1 x 30.

Wednesday
1. Bench press: 3 x 5 progressively heavier warmup sets, then 5 singles with 70% of your one-rep max. Add weight each week until you are handling 90% of your former one-rep max for all 5 singles. (This should occur around week six of the program.) From then on, try to add 5

pounds per week for the final six weeks. Most guys can only add 5 pounds per week for one or two weeks, and then they reduce to 2 pounds a week. Two weeks into the post-90% stage, you can drop to 2-4 heavy singles if you need to do so. Some men get good results from working up to only *one* heavy single. For all your sets, remember to train with a two-second pause on all reps.
2. Pulldown to the chest: 4 x 5.
3. Crunch sit-up with a dumbbell on the chest: 1 x 30.

Friday
1. Deadlift: 4 x 5 (warmups), 2 x 5 heavy.
2. Shrug: 4 x 6.
3. Hammer curl: 4 x 6.
4. Side bend: 1 x 30 (30 per side using a heavy dumbbell).

"This is a pretty straight-forward routine," said Flynn. "It's a variation of the rest-pause training system featured in Peary Rader's Iron Man back in the pre-steroid days, when guys still knew how to train intelligently. It still gets written up from time to time in HARDGAINER."

"But it sounds too simple to work."

"You are darn right it's simple," said Flynn. "You don't need complex routines to get good results. The best routines in the world are the simple, straight-forward programs. No fancy equipment, no computerized set/rep/weight plans, and no exotic supplements. Nothing that claims to be the latest thing from Bulgaria, and nothing you can't pronounce. It's the basics that do the job, every time—there's no magic and no mystery."

"I was just kidding," I mumbled. "How long did you keep the kid on the third program?" Flynn told me that Charlie stayed on the program for three twelve-week cycles, with a one-week break after each cycle. After the first cycle, he had increased his top lift to 280 pounds. At the end of the second cycle, he hit 290 pounds. At the end of the third cycle, the kid was dying to try a 300-pound lift. But Flynn told him he couldn't try a PR in the gym—he had to save it for competition.

"Competition!" screamed the kid. "I want to max out now!"

"Max out on Saturday," said Flynn. He handed the kid a flyer for a drug-free bench press contest in Central City. The kid was flabbergasted—Flynn had entered him in the contest and bought him a pair of competition-style wrist wraps and a new bench shirt, sized to fit him perfectly.

"I'd love to be there cheering you on," said Flynn, "but I have this crazy friend who's getting married and no matter what I say to talk him out of it, he's bound and determined to go through with the thing. I have to be in church while you are having fun at the power meet."

"So what happened?" I asked.

"It was a real tragedy," Flynn answered. "He got married."

"No, I mean what happened at the meet!" I shouted.

"Exactly what I expected," Flynn answered. "The kid took first place in the pure-novice division of the bench press competition. Did 260 on his opener, took 280 for his second attempt and won with his third lift—an easy 300. Then he tried a fourth attempt and hit 315—which demonstrated the extra kick he got from his support gear and proves why you are better off saving the gear for competition or for the infrequent occasions when you attempt a new personal record in the gym. The 315 was a new state record for novice lifters and Charlie jumped up and down about a dozen times after he made the lift. Remember, this was a strict, competition lift with a pause at the chest. Compare that to the 180 pounds he had been stuck at for a full year before he came here for enlightenment—and that 180 lift was a touch-and-go rep with an arch and his butt three inches off the bench."

"So what's next on the agenda for the Bench Press King?" I asked.

"Well," said Flynn, "he enjoyed the bench press meet so much that he's asked me for a specialization program for the squat and deadlift. Seems he doesn't just want to be good at the bench press. The kid wants to be a full-fledged powerlifter. I can't wait to map out his training program." □

HOW TO JOIN THE 400-POUND CLUB

If you have turned to the advanced routines before reading what went before, this is a program of at least eighteen months or so for men who can already bench press at least 300 pounds. To get to this 300-pound level, you *must* stick with programs like those described in the first part of this course. Save the advanced program for the time when you are truly advanced.

There I was, innocently minding my own business, when I got a call from Stuart McRobert asking for an article on bench press training for really advanced guys—those of you out there who have already made it over the 300-pound mark and are shooting for 350 or even 400.

"Call Kubik," I told Stuart.

"Kubik's on vacation, Flynn," said Stuart. "My publishing deadline is coming up and you are my only hope!"

Anyhow, here's the low-down on bench press training for advanced guys. I have a system that I use at my gym—invariably with great success. It even worked for Kubik—the guy used to be a scrawny lawyer with goggles for glasses, an affinity for Latin phrases, and an average bench press. Kubik still quotes Latin and still has goggles for glasses, but he's now a double-bodyweight bench presser in drug-free competition.

First, you need to realize that advanced training on the bench press is hardly mysterious or exotic. What it basically calls for is lots of time and patience. Throw in a bushel or two of common sense and loads of hard work, and you have all of the ingredients for a 350 or perhaps even a 400-pound bench press if you have a good body structure for pressing.

Plenty has been written about bench pressing for advanced men—most of it is utter hogwash. You don't need complicated, computerized training programs, nor do you need the latest in Eastern European sports medicine. All you need to do is train in a sensible, progressive fashion.

A great bench press requires incredibly strong pecs, delts and triceps, and heavy upper back development. Most guys try to train all four of these muscle groups extra hard in order to increase their overall benching power. This strategy, however, just doesn't work for an advanced man, particularly an advanced hard gainer. The heavy weights that an advanced man is capable of handling will quickly lead to overwork if you try to specialize on four muscle groups at the same time.

In my system, you plan your program so that the first phase emphasizes chest development, the second stresses the shoulders, the third highlights tricep development, the fourth emphasizes the upper back, and the fifth focuses on concentrated work leading to an absolute maximum single. You increase your benching power one segment at a time, then you put it all together and blow away your former personal record. Works every time—if I knew a decent lawyer, I would patent the program.

GENERAL PRINCIPLES

I train my advanced men on a five-phase cycle. Each phase of the cycle lasts twelve weeks, except for the final phase which lasts for twenty weeks. You take a one week's break—no barbell exercise at all—after each phase of the cycle. During each one-week layoff you can jog, bicycle, swim, chase girls or go fishing—just stay out of the gym. That's important. This means the whole program takes about eighteen months to complete, and perhaps longer if you spread the workouts out more; but remember, nothing worth having ever comes fast. It takes a long time to develop a great bench press. The guys who claim they can add 50 pounds to an advanced lifter's bench press in ten weeks are out to con you.

For the first four phases, use a sensible training cycle where you use relatively light weights during the first workout, and progressively add weight from workout to workout until you are handling poundages that really make you strain to get your reps, sometime around the sixth week or so of the program. *At that point, keep the weights constant in all of your exercises other than the regular bench press and the exercises for the particular body part you are emphasizing in each cycle.* (These movements are italicized in each program so you will know what they are.) On these exercises, start light, work up to a heavy poundage by week number six, then try to add 5 pounds to the bar every week for the duration of the training cycle. If that's too much, add just 2 pounds. Get some small discs to be able to do this.

On the final bench press day in each twelve-week cycle, try a new max in the bench press. Do 2 progressively heavier warmup sets (5 reps per set), then do singles. Work up to 10 or 15 pounds under your former best, then try 5 pounds *more* than your former best. If you manage the new PR without too much difficulty, try another single with 10 or even 15 pounds over your former max. A former 350-pound bencher might try 135 x 5, 225 x 5, 275 x 1, 315 x 1, 335 x 1, 355 x 1, and 360 or 365 x 1, depending on how the 355 feels. Your goal is to increase your max by 5-15 pounds at the end of each twelve-week cycle. That may not sound like much, but it's an increase of 25-75 pounds after completing the full, five-phase program.

When in the final stage of *any* program, cycle or phase, regardless of whether you are using an advanced or non-advanced routine, you *must* pile on extra rest and sleep, and increase your intake of nutritious food. The final part of a cycle is the "new territory" stage, and you *must* supply the rest, sleep and food components in abundance if you are to make the best gains you can.

The suggested routines don't involve many exercises, sets or reps, but that does *not* mean you can rush through them. Power training requires *long* rests between sets—3-5 minutes between your heavy sets is about right for most guys. Some top lifters rest even longer (up to ten minutes between very heavy sets). If you try to race through these programs, you are cheating yourself. Also, if you need to pause for a few breaths between reps during your heavy sets, feel free to do so. Continuous tension reps, or "counting the seconds," are the last things you need if you want to push the most iron you possibly can. You must *drive* the bar upward as hard and forcefully as possible, in *perfect* form. Driving the bar up does *not* mean cheating and throwing the weights around and, eventually, getting yourself injured. Successful long-term training necessitates avoiding injuries—so don't do anything that exposes you to inevitable injury.

Heavy leg and back work—especially heavy squats and deadlifts—is included in the bench press specialization. Hard work on the squat and deadlift stimulates the natural production of testosterone, thereby helping to build strength and muscle throughout the body. Too many lifters who specialize on the bench press do little or no serious squatting or deadlifting. All serious benchers should squat and/or deadlift hard and heavy, unless injuries or structural limitations prevent this.

I know some of you have problems squatting and deadlifting. The correct form for each movement is covered in the book BRAWN, and also gets covered regularly in HARDGAINER. The magazine also keeps you up to date with good alternative movements, including information for guys with access to some of the newer machines designed to work the thighs and hips.

There is much important detail on the how-to and how-not-to of exercise performance that can't be included in a single course like this one. BRAWN, while not being exhaustive, provides much of this detail and, in combination with personal experience or a *good* instructor, will keep you training safely and injury free.

Always keep in mind that we are all different. Some of you will find that these programs tire you out and leave you feeling drained and overtrained, even though you are genuinely an advanced bencher. Feel free to *reduce* the workload by cutting back on the number of sets or by eliminating exercises. This will be the key to success for at least 50% of you. (It's so important that we will include special instructions about an abbreviated version at the end of the description of each training cycle.) Rest and recuperation are critical factors for an advanced lifter. Some of you may do better by taking ten days to complete each of the three workouts in any phase of the program, instead of the usual one-week period. That's fine—the extra days of rest may prove to be just what you need to keep the gains coming.

If you have a shoulder problem, feel free to wear a bench shirt on all of your sets of regular benches. If, however, you do wear a shirt when you train, you need to be careful not to let the shirt do the work for you. Do *not* drop the bar and use the shirt for a rebound effect. Lower the bar slowly and under control, and *pause* briefly at the bottom of each rep. Also, wear a shirt that's old and a bit loose—or else buy a shirt for training that's a size too large. If you compete, keep two shirts—one for meets and a looser one for training, (but you can use the tighter shirt in the gym on the rare occasions when you go for a PR).

PHASE ONE:
Building the Chest

The first phase stresses development of the chest muscles, while still providing plenty of work for the rest of the body.

Monday
1. *Regular-grip bench press*: 5 or 6 triples, starting light and working up to your top weight for 3 reps, then doing a second set with 10 pounds less. Do each rep with a pause at the chest. Reg Park, one of the all-time great bodybuilders, and a 500-pound bench presser, credited the pause-style bench press with giving him *both* enormous strength *and* terrific chest development. Use at least the same length of pause used in competition. A powerlifting judge will require you to pause until the bar is completely motionless. (If you lower the bar slowly and under control, you *reduce* the time it takes for the bar to come to a full stop, and thus get a quicker press command than if you drop the bar to your chest.) When training, hold the bar at the chest for at least one second. Two seconds will work better for some of you—this is what Park used. Be sure to stay "tight"—like a coiled spring—at the bottom position and *explode* the bar upward. The pause-tension-explosion is what will build your pecs. This is a very stressful way to train, so be sure you adhere strictly to the general advice to start each cycle with comfortable weights (in all exercises) and take six weeks or so before pushing your hardest.
2. *Low-incline dumbbell press*: 5 sets of 5-8 reps (2 progressive warmups and then 3 heavy sets). Work for a good, controlled stretch across the pectorals—but don't exaggerate the stretch or else you will be asking for shoulder problems. George Eiferman, a Mr. America winner from the pre-steroid era, had the best chest development of any bodybuilder in the world at one time. The incline dumbbell press was his primary exercise for building his pecs. I suggest you use a 30^0 angle—but if that doesn't feel right, try a different angle.
3. Pulldown to the chest (medium grip, parallel if possible): 5-6 sets, starting with a light weight and working up to your heaviest weight for 6 reps.

Wednesday
1. Parallel squat: 6 x 3 reps, starting light and working up to your top triple.
2. Seated military press: 4 x 5. Work up to 90% of your top weight for 5 reps. Don't go too heavy on this movement or you will compromise

your bench press training during phase one. In phase two you will train your shoulders as heavy as possible.
3. Standing barbell curl: 4 x 6-8, starting light and working up to your top weight on the final set.
4. Calf raise: 2 x 20-30 (use the standing or seated version, whichever you prefer).

Friday
1. Deadlift from the knees: 6 x 3. Start light and work up to your top weight for 3 reps.
2. *Regular-grip bench press*: Same as Monday but use only 80% of the weights used then.
3. *Low-incline barbell press*, beginning each rep from a dead stop. Use a power rack to do these. Do 5 sets of 6 reps—3 warmup sets and 2 heavy sets.
4. Side bend and crunch sit-up: 1 x 20-30 for each movement.
5. Any gripping exercise you happen to favor—2 sets per hand. Pinch-gripping heavy plates, or hanging from a chinning bar for as long as possible, are good movements.

If the workload is too great for you, try an abbreviated version of the program. On Monday, do 5 progressively heavier triples in the bench press (as in the regular program), but do only 2 sets of 5 reps in the low-incline dumbbell press and the pulldown. On Wednesday, do 5 sets of 3 reps in the squat, skip the presses and calf work, and do 2 sets of 5 reps in the curls. On Friday, do 5 sets of 3 in the deadlift from the knees, 2 sets of military presses, one set of crunches, and nothing else. After week six, train squats heavy one week and deadlifts light, then deadlifts heavy and squats light the following week, and alternate in this fashion for the remainder of the program.

PHASE TWO:
Building the Shoulders

After completing phase one, take a one-week break, then go to phase two, which emphasizes your shoulders.

Monday
1. *Regular bench press*, 5 x 5 (do 4 progressively heavier warmup sets and use your top weight for 5 reps on your final set). Do touch-and-go reps during this second phase, not pause reps.
2. Pulldown or bent-over row: 4 x 6-8, starting light and working up to your top weight for your final set.
3. *Seated dumbbell press*, preferably on an 80°-incline bench: 5 x 5, working up to your top set for 5 reps.
4. *Power rack press from eye level*, performed in a power rack, standing or seated; push the bar from eye level to a lockout: 5 sets of 3 reps, working up to your top weight for 3 reps.

Wednesday
1. Parallel squat: 5 sets of 6 reps, working up to your top weight on your final set.
2. Calf raise (standing): 2 x 20-30.
3. Crunch sit-up: 1 x 20-30.
4. Side bend: 1 x 20-30 (each side).
5. Any gripping exercise you like: 1 or 2 sets. Try attaching a three-inch pipe to your chinning bar and hang from the pipe for as long as possible. Benchers *need* a strong grip.

Friday
1. Deadlift: 5 x 6, working up to your top weight for 6 reps.
2. *80°-incline press* performed in the power rack; start each rep from a dead stop at the bottom pins and push the bar to lockout: 6 x 3, working up to your top set for 3 reps.
3. *Push press*: use a strong knee drive to get the bar going and push it overhead without moving your feet; lock the bar vigorously and lower slowly to the starting position, emphasizing the negative portion of the movement on each rep; 5 x 5, working up to your top set for 5 reps.
4. Alternate dumbbell curl or standing barbell curl: 3 x 6-8, working up to your top weight for your final set.
5. Same gripping exercise as on Wednesday: one set only.

Remember to start light and take six weeks to build back to your best poundages. Then, hold all lifts constant except in the italicized movements where you forge into new poundage ground for the final six weeks of the phase. Finally, try a new bench press maximum single as described earlier.

For an abbreviated version of the second phase, try doing benches and pulldowns on Monday, squats and crunches on Wednesday, and deadlifts and 80°-incline presses and curls on Friday (same sets and reps for each exercise as in the regular routines). Alternate heavy and light weeks in the squat and deadlift after the sixth week of the program (see instructions for the abbreviated program for the first phase).

PHASE THREE:
Building the Triceps

The third phase of this advanced training program calls for extra attention to your triceps.

Monday
1. *Regular bench press*: 5 x 5, starting light and working up to your top weight for 5 reps, followed by 4 singles with 10-30 pounds more than your top 5-rep weight. Do touch-and-go reps on the 5-rep sets and pause-style reps on the singles.
2. Pulldown or chin: 5 x 6, adding weight each set and working up to your top weight for 6 reps.
3. *Close-grip bench press*: 5 x 6, same procedure as on the pulldown or chin. Hands should be about 16" apart.
4. Any grip exercise you favor: 2 sets per arm. For a great article on grip work, see HARDGAINER, March 1993.

Wednesday
1. Parallel squat: 5 x 5, working up to your top weight for one set of 5 reps.
2. Standing or seated calf raise: 3 x 15.
3. Standing barbell curl: 3 x 6, working up to your top weight for 6 reps.
4. Crunch sit-up: 2 x 20-40, holding a weight on your chest for resistance.

Friday
1. Deadlift: 5 x 5, working up to your top weight for 5 reps.
2. *Close-grip bench press in the power rack*. Set the pins 2-3" above your chest, use a grip about 16" between your thumbs, and do 5 progressively heavier triples, followed by 2 sets of 5 reps with 30 pounds under your top weight for the triples.
3. *Alternate dumbbell press* (standing or seated): 5 x 6, doing 2 progressively heavier warmup sets and 3 sets at your top weight. Flex the tricep *hard* as you lock out each rep on this exercise.
4. Side bend: 2 x 20-30 per side.
5. Grip work: same as Monday.

As with the other phases, start easy and take six weeks to return to your best poundages. Then, hold all poundages constant except in the bench press and the tricep exercises, which you push into new poundage ground over the next six weeks. End the phase with another new bench press max.

For the abbreviated version of this program, do benches and close grips on Monday (same sets and reps as in the basic program), do squats and curls on Wednesday (using the same sets and reps as in the basic program), and limit the Friday workout to deadlifts, close-grip benches in the rack, a set of crunches, and nothing else. Alternate heavy and light weeks on the squat and deadlift (as in the first phase).

PHASE FOUR:
Building the Back

The fourth phase calls for extra work on the upper back muscles, i.e., the muscles which form a cushion for your bench pressing. One of the best ways to develop benching strength is to pay extra attention to your upper back development. It assists the elbows-against-the-lats pressing technique (see pages 7 and 8) that's important for benching your best. This is a little known facet of bench press training that has proven to be invaluable for those who have given it a try.

Monday
1. *Deadlift from the knees*: 6 x 5, working up to your top weight for 2 sets of 5 reps.
2. *Shrug*: same as for the deadlift.
3. *Regular bench press*: 6 x 5, same as for the deadlift. Pause briefly on all reps.
4. Close-grip bench press (16" between thumbs): 2 x 6-8 using your top weight on each set.
5. Grip work: 2 sets of any heavy gripping movement, or just hang for as long as possible from a chinning bar with a towel wrapped around it.

Wednesday
1. Seated military press: 5 x 6 (work up to your top weight for 2 sets of 6 reps).
2. *Pulldown to the chest*: 5 x 8-10 (do 2 progressively heavier warmup sets and then 3 work sets).
3. *Wide-grip chins*: do 2 sets of as many reps as possible with bodyweight; work hard and steady, with no dropping, no bouncing, and no cheating.
4. *One-arm dumbbell row*: 2 sets per arm for 8-10 reps per set, using the same poundage for each set.

Friday
1. Parallel squat: 6 x 5 (work up to approximately 20 pounds under your top weight for 5 reps and do 2 sets with that weight).
2. Standing calf raise: 2 x 20-30.
3. Seated calf raise: 2 x 15-20.
4. Hammer curl: 3 x 8-10 (work up to your top weight for your final set).
5. Stiff-legged deadlift: do one set of 20 reps with 50% of your bodyweight—this is intended *solely* to stretch and loosen your lower back muscles. Use the same weight for the entire phase.

As with the other phases, only push into new poundage territory in the focus (italicized) lifts during the final six weeks, i.e., the regular bench press and the back exercises for this phase. Keep the other lifts at the week-six poundage for the rest of the phase. Try for a new bench press max on the last day of the fourth phase.

For an abbreviated version of the fourth program, do exercises 1, 2 and 3 on the Monday schedule, exercises 1 and 2 in the Wednesday workout, and exercise 1 plus a single set of crunches in the Friday session. After week six, train your squats with medium poundages one week and heavy poundages the next—this will help keep you from overtraining your lower back. Use the same set/rep patterns in the abbreviated version as in the basic program.

PHASE FIVE:
Hitting a Big New Max

The final phase of your training program takes the extra strength that you have built in your chest, shoulder, tricep and upper back muscles and blends it together for a big new maximum in the bench press. Do five four-week mini-cycles for this phase. During the first week of each mini-cycle, do 5 reps on all of your sets of regular bench presses. During the second week of each mini-cycle, do 3 reps on each set of your regular bench presses. During the third week of the mini-cycle, do 2 progressively heavier sets of 5 reps as a warmup, then do singles, taking big jumps and working your way up to about 95% of your previous one-rep max. Depending on your strength levels and how you space your poundage jumps, you should do a total of between 4 and 7 single reps during this training session. A guy who benches 380 might do 135 x 5, 225 x 5, 275 x 1, 325 x 1, 350 x 1, and 360 x 1. You will feel plenty strong on these sets, so use perfect form. Don't try to exceed your former max, however; save that for week four. (That's important, no matter how strong you feel. You can't expect to make consistent gains if you constantly try for a new max.)

For the fourth week of the first mini-cycle, try working up to a new max. Use an approach similar to that used in week three. Our hypothetical 380-pound bencher should try something like 135 x 5, 225 x 5, 315 x 1, 350 x 1, 370 x 1 and 385 or 390 for a new PR.

For week number five, start a new mini-cycle with 5 reps on the bench press, and then proceed from week to week as in the first mini-cycle.

You will be training your bench press hard and heavy for twenty consecutive weeks on this final phase, or longer if you spread the three workouts over more days than the given one-week period. You work up to your top weight for 5 reps in week one, your top weight for a triple in week two, and so on as given below. As an advanced man, you will be able to handle this load, but *only* if you hold back on your other exercises. Use a standard cycling approach on squats, deadlifts, pulldowns and the other scheduled movements. Start with relatively light weights and gradually build back to your top weights after six weeks or so. Then go back down to lighter poundages and repeat the process for a further six weeks or so, and then drop the weights and go through the process for a third time. *Don't* try to combine twenty weeks of concentrated benching with twenty weeks of full-bore work on your other exercises. It won't work.

The entire final phase looks like this:

Monday
1. Regular bench press:
   Week #1 of each mini cycle
   5-7 sets of 5 reps, working up to your top weight for a single set of 5 reps.
   Week #2 of each mini cycle
   5-7 sets of 3 reps, working up to your top weight for a single set of 3 reps.
   Week #3 of each mini cycle
   5-7 sets, starting with 2 progressively heavier warmup sets of 5 reps per set and then doing singles until you work up to about 95% of your former one-rep max.
   Week #4 of each mini cycle
   The same as week #3, but go after a new maximum.
2. Dumbbell incline press (30⁰ incline) *or* close-grip bench press (16" grip):
   4 x 5-8, starting light and working up to your heaviest weight for your final set. Do this work *only* in weeks one and two of each mini-cycle.
3. Pulldown: 4 x 5-8, starting light and working up to your heaviest weight for your final set.

Wednesday
1. Parallel squat: 6 x 3 (do 4 progressively heavier warmup sets and 2 sets of 3 reps with 10 or 20 pounds less than your top weight for a triple).
2. Standing calf raise: 4 x 12-15 (same weight on each set).
3. Crunch sit-up: 1 x 20-30 (hold a weight on your chest for resistance).

Friday
1. Deadlift from the knees: 5 x 5 (do 4 progressively heavier warmup sets and use your top weight on your final set).
2. Seated press behind neck: same as for the deadlift. Do this pressing movement *only* in weeks one and two of each mini-cycle.
3. Standing barbell curl: same as for the deadlift.
4. Barbell reverse curl: 4 x 15 (do 2 progressively heavier warmup sets and 2 sets with your top weight for 15 reps).
5. Any gripping exercise: 2 sets.

For a more abbreviated version, do nothing but benches and 2 sets of pulldowns on Monday. Take your second workout on Thursday, doing squats, curls (2 x 6-8) and crunches the first week, and squats, deadlifts, curls and crunches the following week. On the week when you squat and deadlift on the same day, only do your warmup sets in the squat.

There you have it. Short, sweet and simple, and straight from the horse's own mouth. I just hope Kubik stays on an extra-long vacation—this writing business is kind of fun. Best of luck to all of you, and if you are ever in our neck of the woods, stop by and take a free workout at Flynn's Gym. Remember, we are the gym that emphasizes heavy iron over designer training apparel.

[Note by Stuart McRobert: The foregoing is in Flynn's own words. Kubik tried to edit it but we wouldn't let him.]

[Note by Kubik: I have researched the issue and I can't sue either of them. Truth is an absolute defense to a defamation claim, so Flynn and Stuart are safe for now. Do try our program though—it *works*.] ▫